The Ninth Wave

Josie-Anne Gray

With thanks to Nick Triplow

Published by Moonfruit Books 2015

5 Crake Avenue

Grimsby

DN33 3NB

ISBN 978-0-9573849-7-2

Cover illustration by Helen Nicholson

Humber Fort painting by Terry Clarke

Printed by GSB Print and Design Ltd

List of Contents

Haile Fort by Terry Clarke

The Ninth Wave

Josie-Anne Gray

'Lady,' he said, 'will you tell me anything about your business?'

'I will, between me and God,' she said. 'My main purpose was to try and see you.'

The First Branch, The Mabinogion.
Translated by Sioned Davies

Foreword

The Ninth Wave is a dramatic re-imagining of the story of Pwyll and Rhiannon initially told in the First Branch of *The Mabinogion,* the great cycle of Welsh myths and tales that has endured down the centuries and fascinates to this day.

The poem relocates the story to the Humber Estuary and the salt marshes at Humberston, North East Lincolnshire, extending south towards the village of Tetney. It is set in a dystopian near future at a time of global crisis and conflict. I have honoured the myth and its origins, retaining Welsh names to create a feeling of dislocation and unfamiliarity which enriches the sense of otherness of the piece.

1

The characters of Rhiannon and Pwyll are brought together by Lord Arawn of *Annwn*, the Otherworld. Pwyll is a man of his time and context, whereas Rhiannon is an immortal, a Goddess absent from this mortal realm for centuries. Arawn is also an immortal, but takes a paternal interest in Pwyll's affairs.

In the original tale, Rhiannon took on the archetype of the calumniated woman; she endured humiliation and suffering that ended in reconciliation with her husband. In this version, events take a different course and the story departs from the motifs and motivations of the original, re-imagining the influence of a damaged and broken world, and questioning whether, as tradition would have us believe, love still holds the answers.

Josie-Anne Gray, 2015

Prelude

In the first quarter of the third millennium
Pwyll is king of the eastern sea.
Britain is ripped and ruined by war;
divisions are rife, blood feuds bitter,
Pwyll adjudges as royal arbiter.

Humankind has forged desolation
desecration and despair,
agony and alienation.
The world is ravaged beyond repair.

Rival warlords seize control
marking territories, building walls.
Old kings command new realms.
Pwyll brokers uneasy peace,
brings the bloodshed to a cease.

Lord Arawn of Annwn rides with Pwyll,
lent to this land for a year and a day.
They sail the creeks that deceive and kill,
fight for each other, outwit death,
feel the east wind steal their breath.

Pwyll and Arawn break colts on the beach,
make their presence heard and seen.
Out in the water on Haile Fort
Pwyll's soldiers guard the river;
note every ripple, every shiver.

Asleep and out of mortal reach,
Rhiannon dreams of wild green hills,
clear air and mountain streams.
The love of men is long forgotten
but now Lord Arawn stirs the cauldron.

Rhiannon's eyes slowly open.

Waking

Rhiannon

> I dream of blue eyes
> I dream of cold eyes
> I dream of someone
> I drown in someone.

> I swirl and turn
> as part of the eddy
> borne on the current.
> The wave builds,
> the water swells.
> I pulse and thrum,
> ride over wrecks
> and the salt-washed
> bones of the dead at rest,
> claimed by the fog,
> malign spirit of the east.

> I hush my mare,
> she whinnies,
> her hackles rise.
> She flashes her whites
> and rears to leap.
> Ripples carry soul whispers
> along the river.
> So many, so many dead.

We're coming in,
we're coming in.

A beam of light
heralds the dawn.
I am new-born,
my eyes open,
my long sleep gone.

In my dream
there were blue eyes
there were cold eyes
there was someone.
Him.

Chorus

Out of the darkness and into the light
Rhiannon ascends on a horse of white.
Up through the waves where she lay dreaming,
up through the mist of the early morning.
Out of the darkness and into the light
Rhiannon ascends on a horse of white.
See her return from the world of the dead,
red hair streams from her sovereign head.
Called from the dreamtime, called to the light,
Rhiannon ascends on a horse of white.
Rhiannon
Rhiannon
Rhiannon

In the Water

Pwyll and Arawn

Pwyll: There was something in the water.
      We rode out to Haile Sand at low tide,
      climbed the tower, kept watch,
      stayed for the swell, the smack of the sea.
      I saw something move the water,
      felt stabbed in the gut.
      My martial instincts ignited,
      there was something in the water.
      We rode out along the bank
      at moon rise. Sea on the left,
      land on the right,
      stared at the water deathly black.
      Saw something break the surface -

Arawn: It's only if you dream that you'll see her
      with her red hair and her white mare.
      You're a loyal friend and brother,
      now I'll give you some advice:
      She's coming from the waves; she's in the water -

Pwyll: There was something in the water.
      We watched all night,
      listened, but the damned wind
      drove me half crazy by three -
      the *witching hour*. Old wives' tales perhaps
      but the hairs on my neck bristled.
      I swear I heard a voice.

Arawn: She'll lead you away from your world
through the veils of all you thought you knew.
Go and meet her on your shore
when dawn light turns to blue.

Pwyll: There *was* something in the water.
I can't think about anything else.
I saw a white horse,
an unkindness of ravens circling.
I heard a silver laugh that got me hard
I'm out of my head -

Arawn: It's only when you dare that you'll meet her
with her red hair and her white mare.
Out of the darkness and into the light,
Rhiannon's coming
when the night's over.
You'll hear her, you'll see her;
but only if you dare brother,
Only if you dare ...

The Lover

Pwyll

In the cold light of an autumn dawning
my heart aches as I fight with a dream
that keeps me wakeful, worried, fretting.
I see her there, her red hair streaming
wild like the white horse she rides through the water,
crashing to my world from the ninth wave.
> God knows, I know she'll be trouble
> and I see myself as clear as day
> with my scarred face and broken soul
> shattering all her dreams in one fell swoop.
> Arawn said, 'Take flowers, build a bower
> protect her from the sea.'
There is nothing to do but let her come
with her eyes turned blind by the rising sun.

At First Sight

Rhiannon

Once I was promised to one I could not love
and rode far from home to rid myself
of a daughter's duty.
My father still rants and rails at my sisters.
There will be no warm sheets or welcoming arms
should I go home.

Here are flowers. Michaelmas daisies
like soft bruises named for an angel,
blood red cyclamen for labour and goodbyes,
late dog rose for protection from wolves,
gladioli swords for battle
and lavender for wounds,
all bound in victorious nasturtium
and tendrils of clinging ivy.

My mare snorts hot breath,
hoofs her disapproval.
'She doesn't like me,' Pwyll says.
His voice makes my veins throb.
I will not swoon like a common girl
but I stumble and he catches me,
lays me on a bed of moss.

Taking Her

Pwyll

She comes as Arawn said she would
and falls into my arms without a thought.
My mouth on her breasts tastes of home.
She pulls me deep inside and I am lost.
The paleness of her skin suggests death.
Something wicked stirs within.
> Should I refuse this love that she demands,
> refuse this so-called gift that asks so much?
> Arawn's words cut like the eastern wind,
> 'A king, a man needs a woman, needs a wife.'
> I could hold her for a while and know no peace,
> then resume that which I trust, the soldier's life.
I slip away and leave her as she sleeps,
go to my own cold bed and there I weep.

Shivering Dawn

Rhiannon

I wake shivering at dawn
turn under the moss blanket
find him gone.
The faintest scent remains.
The bank is bathed in dank sea fog
the wind has bite.
I clothe myself in wings,
take flight, circle Haile Sand.
His men sleep.
He is beyond my reach.

I take claw vengeance
on field creatures,
rip them from nests
chew them to the marrow,
leave pellets.
Blood and tears streak
my face as the sun breaks cloud.
I alight on amassed deaths,
small bones and broken wings.
Still cold, I keep my feathers
matted with the mess of slaughter,
cast a salt ring round my head
to keep myself unseen.

The day spends itself in pacing,
watching the air for signs of him.
At sunset my feet bleed,
I stand in the tide,
howl at the sting.

I mix blood and spit,
draw in sand,
conjure a dark wind,
find the path to his head,
catch his dream in my net.

Chorus

An unkindness of ravens caws at Pwyll
riding to Annwn on galloping colt,
pursued by an owl in soundless flight
he flees the darkness, seeks the light;

finds an oak in a dappled glade,
lays his head on cooling grass,
his mind disturbed by night's dark heat
and a vision in which lovers meet.

Reverie

Rhiannon

Place your hand on my breast
and there will be flowers beneath your touch.
You've been inside me, now you leave me,
but the fire in your eyes defies the cold.
I can bring down rain in moonlight
and the moon herself will weep for me.

You walk through this dream
wearing your field armour.
You will not hold me by the hand.
You will not sweep me up in a dance.
You will not feed me from your plate.
You will not clothe me in the robes of state.
You will not kiss me before the world.

But you will come back to burn me
and you will leave again at dawn.

In Her World

Pwyll

When I leave her will I break her heart?
The love she bears brings neither of us good.
I want to see her rise above the hurt
and ride her white horse back into the waves.
She came to me with sunlight in her eyes
but in her arms I only feel the moon,
its watery pull drags me down so low
I fear I'll never see light again.
        Poison ivy, sleepy lavender and roses
        have induced in me this deep narcotic lust,
        I cannot love this woman and I know it;
        there's something of the witch in her dark touch.
I'll go to her again and tell the truth,
let her go and free both of us.

Revelation

Rhiannon

The Major Arcana
    First card – The Fool.
    This is you as you are now
    at this time of our meeting.
    You don't see your true state.
    All your mirrors are black
    reflecting back the past.
    But we are all fools.
    I breathe deeply,
    hold for a long count,
    hold until it hurts,
    take my mind to the quiet place
    where the fog clears.
    Begin.

A crescent moon lay; one simple question.
The Minor Arcana. Threes. Swords.
    Your bleeding heart.
    You sleep, uneasily.
    This is the card of the dark hour
    the one before dawn.
    I see you turn away from me.
    Now you are gone.

The Minor Arcana. Threes. Cups.
    The maidens dance amid
    abundance. Your kingdom thrives.

There is peace and plenty.
You won a hard victory,
I ask too much of you.
I see you turn away from me.
Now you are gone.

The Minor Arcana. Threes. Wands.
The Mage turns his back too.
He is complete, resolved.
His future is defined;
in it I am pure absence.
I see you turn away from me.
Now you are gone.

The Major Arcana. The Moon.
She rises with all three faces.
I know her and her tears too well.
Dear night, home of rest and dream.
Illusion is hers, she has no time
for logic and reason.
I see you turn away from me.
Now you are gone.

One more. Bad luck to break the pattern.
Just one more.

The Major Arcana. The Sun. Inverse.
You brighten my darkness
then obliterate me. You lay all to waste
to impose order. You burn down

my columns and cloisters,
level them as my head pounds
and the forest wolf howls.
A ring of blood circles my bone moon.
A red moon – always trouble.
Water laps at the hem of my gown,
cools my feet
lures me down.

Breathe. Breathe. *Breathe*.
Follow the sun.
His rays wound, burn my brow.
I have no shield,
I cry to the moon,
my sodden wings
cannot take me in flight
to her still pools
to where I might cool my cheek
against her marble breast.

I love him; it is a simple thing,
but poison to him, so it seems.
Drink me and let the night blaze,
let wet heat take us both.
The wave is building
out at sea.
Mortal time is short.

Two Kings

Pwyll and Arawn

Arawn: Hail brother, well met by moonlight,
      my hounds are ready for a hunt by night.
      But I see you carry trouble, the hounds can wait.

Pwyll: She was your gift, I cannot take her
      too much of the dark is in her.

Arawn: You held back for a year and a day.
      My woman told me of your restraint.
      This one is all yours.
      Take her, have her with my blessing.

Pwyll: I have had her and I will again
      tonight under this blood moon.
      I'll bed her in that bower
      but tomorrow brother ...

Arawn: Tomorrow. Today. Yesterday.
      To me they are all one.
      Go to her. Bed her.
      For God's sake try to love her.

Pwyll: We will hunt again in your realm and mine.
      Don't think me ungrateful
      I am king of the day.

Arawn: And Rhiannon is the queen of night.

Wretched

Pwyll

I wake on a bright cold autumn morning
from a howling dream of an angel falling.

I kick at leaves and rail at indiscretion,
plan the path towards one last seduction.

I see the road before me broken, bent,
and wonder if this was my true intent.

Evening rises and the tired sun squints.
Lines of light across the bed, unsubtle hints.

Sickness born of sorrow rises free
I spit fury at the world and me.

Quickening

Rhiannon

I feel it quicken
white light fractures deep within.
It gives me no joy.

A child.
A boy.

Chorus

Rhiannon is wrapped in a shawl of mist,
soundless tears sting her eyes.
She stands at the shore, her gaze fixed.
Her cold breath joins the worried air,
the bitter wind pulls at her hair,
the elements make their call on her.

The son in her womb dreams of the father,
holds a royal name close to his heart,
calls to his mother to please have pity,
to let him take his rightful place,
to know the father, to see his face.

Distant Thunder

Rhiannon

I sleep and hear the sound of distant thunder,
rolling in a riot of damning dreams.
I've lost my love; it will not be recovered.
He has moved himself too far away from me.

When I awake he won't be there beside me,
he'll leave the moment sleep touches my brow,
pausing for the briefest hesitation.
Now dark salt water calls me back below.

My heart breaks as others broke before it,
my tears swell like storms far out at sea.
Time will not heal the wound he has inflicted
but soon I will reveal what this pain means.

The time will come when he will feel the cold blade
wounding to the centre of his soul.
Nothing on this earth can give replacement
for the loss he'll feel; the deepest, blackest hole.

Chorus

Rhiannon's birds fly to her call,
fill the air in a whirling merl.
Out on Haile the alarm is raised
as the heat of a threat
raises the hairs
on the back of the neck
of every mother's son.

No man can account
for the source of his terror,
for a feeling of fear
older than time.

Later each will say,
will swear on his life
that he saw that day
a red haired woman
on a horse of white
appear on the water
for the blink of an eye
then disappear from earthly sight.

Lady Sovereignty

Rhiannon

I was Lady Sovereignty
in the centuries of The Great She
when my hand held the balance.
Now is the time of men,
the third millennium of their succession.
They boil God, oil and blood
to no good end.

Beware, beware.
My sisters stir.
Brigid hides her medicine bowl;
Shelagh-na-gig seeks out your babes.
If Morrigan rises
she will turn the earth's crust black.

I am going back to salt,
back to tide,
the dark swell of the deep.
The world will not hear from me
while this state keeps.

Remember me.
Once I was Rhiannon.
Once I was Lady Sovereignty.

Last Time

Pwyll

Picture this: an arch of fragrant roses.
I guide her every step towards my room.
Her senses are delighted with the scene
I have set. She ascends the dark stairs.
I watch her trepidation on the rise,
will her to surrender from the shadows.
This seduction is on my terms, not hers.
I accept it in its frailty and despair.
She lays down for me and I take her gladly.
How can I not when she gives so freely?
> I risk myself once more to have her wholly,
> resolve to leave as morning rises clear.
> Tonight she's mine, tomorrow comes the price.
> All traces of tonight can be washed clean.

Lady of Flight and Feather

Rhiannon

On my wings of silent power
I ride the evening sky
and blend into the twilight
at disappearing day.

Wrapping my feathers
around his uneasy dream
I alight at his window,
breathe in his rose scent.

My keen eye catches every move
as the stillness of the air
settles in my mind
and I see the end.

The lull of cold night air
forces me to rise,
his chest heaves once as tears
brim in the corners of his eyes.

Chorus

Into the darkness and out of the light
Rhiannon descends on a horse of white,
back to the waves with no fear of drowning,
back to the place of eternal dreaming.
Into the darkness and out of the light
Rhiannon descends on a horse of white.
See her return to the world of the dead
red hair streaming from her sovereign head.
Into the darkness and out of the light
Rhiannon descends on a horse of white.

Pwyll

Rhiannon.
  Rhiannon.
    Rhiannon.

Glossary

Pwyll: Lord of Dyfed in the First Branch of *The Mabinogion*. Here he is warlord/king of the eastern cantref of a newly imagined Britain.

Arawn: Lord of Annwn, the Otherworld in Welsh and Celtic mythology. Lord Arawn can be seen hunting with his dogs in this realm on the quarter days of the year.

Rhiannon: one of the great Celtic Goddesses, associated with horses, black birds and protection of the land. She had the power to shape shift and to move between the worlds.

The major and minor arcanas: the imagery in *Revelation* is taken from the original Marseilles Tarot deck of 1499.

Haile Fort: Haile is one of two forts built during the First World War. They sit in the Humber Estuary and are two iconic landmarks of the region.

Acknowledgements

There are several works by other artists and writers that have been influential and inspirational in the production of this work.

The Mabinogion translated by Sioned Davies, Oxford World's Classics

Idylls of the King, Alfred Lord Tennyson, Penguin Classics
The Ninth Wave, Russell Celyn Jones, Seren Books
The Ninth Wave, Kate Bush, EMI Records
Rigantona's Daughters, Susan Garlick and Scott Jasper, Dragonfly Moon Music
The Humber Forts, paintings by Terry Clarke